FINISHING LINE PRESS

www.finishinglinepress.com

Starting Again

poems by

Brian Satrom

Finishing Line Press
Georgetown, Kentucky

Starting Again

Publisher: Leah Maines

Editor: Christen Kincaid

Cover Art: *purplehotel* by Scott Fortino, www.scottfortino.com

Author Photo: Lian Partlow

Cover Design: David Bowen

Printed in the USA on acid-free paper.
Order online: www.finishinglinepress.com
            also available on amazon.com

Author inquiries and mail orders:
Finishing Line Press
P. O. Box 1626
Georgetown, Kentucky 40324
U. S. A.

Table of Contents

For Lian

For Lian

I. Onset of Shadows

Witness

I'm looking for the rattlesnake, which sits there
coiled and dark. But the revelation
is the gopher snake shedding its skin
in the next terrarium, a gradual
easing out of its sheath as if by power
of concentration. What's left behind
brittle, textured. An impression.
When I step through the doors of the nature center
into the sun, my eyes need
a moment to adjust. Then I run to catch up
with you, you and your sister already
starting down the sandy trail
into the arroyo. I don't feel different
except for a sense of lightness from what I've seen.

Aftereffects

I assumed it was just the flu
before it emerged three days later (as if from the shadow

of my assumption) to make itself apparent,
needing me for that,
to tighten its grip around, my chest hurting,

no strength in my lungs,

my fist pounded against the wall an improvised voice
to draw attention.
A condensed sense of space.

The red scar the surgeon's left
on my right side

starts down from my shoulder blade,

a line a child could have drawn with a stick
in fresh cement.

In a casual tone,
as if giving me brief operating instructions
for a new purchase,

he's telling me to massage it to help it heal.

The question I don't know how to phrase
because the thought

seems more superstitious
than real, isn't about what's been cut out
or the physical aftereffects,

but what's unseen, any dark matter the opening up
of my body's let in.

Turning Around

I can wait.
If I pause long enough, shut off the engine,
a hard quiet.

Hot, airless shadows of branches under the creosote bush.
Calcified, cloudless sky.
Drifted sand under our tires.

The ridge on the horizon
no longer a ridge I need to travel to.
I'm trying not to spin the wheels when I start up again,

the backend sliding when I do.
Your point well taken about the barrenness
of what's in the distance in deserts

even if we were to reach it
(notice me agreeing now,
having lost the certainty that brought me here).

Behind us
the paved road out of reach on foot
in this soft sand,

an underlying need, not yet panic,
to get us turned around
and headed back on the one-lane trail.

I shift into drive and then reverse,
looking for the right touch on the pedal, taking
whatever traction I can get.

Tule Lake

Site of the WWII internment camp for Japanese Americans

The shush of cars and trucks on 139.

Martha, it was your idea
the four of us drive down, you our curiosity,
our conscience.

As if there's something to summon from this place,

the past could leave an imprint, coming here
we're closer to it.

Castle Rock less a castle, more like the superstructure

of a ship sailing out.
The openness a contradiction.
Sunlight harsh on the eyes.

No lake.

I'd have been
like anyone driving by back then
heading somewhere else,

relieved I had
what I had, the freedom to keep going.

There's nothing left of the camp.
Just a concrete shell of a building
and a plaque,

though down the street, not sure at first
we trust our sight,

what looks like a small re-creation

complete with fencing and barbed wire,
a compound of gray shacks,
freshly painted, for migrant field hands,

this arid landscape
morphing into a dreamscape

where structures emerge we've never seen before

but seem to know,
familiar enough, even part of us.

America

What's it like? I get the question
on the playground and hesitate, already

the details slipping because it's been a while,
though I still have the accent.

When I lived there last I didn't think about
what it was like living there. So my memory

a residue of summer light, smog, hot sidewalks
on bare feet, skateboards, sometimes, on lucky

occasions, the ocean, a tidal pool,
wet swimming trunks, salt on the air, on my tongue.

And not yet desire, longing, emptiness
taking shape. But no words

for all that. So I've refined the trick
of not answering right away, letting

the questioner imagine, fill in blanks.
It's bigger, isn't it? Yes, I say. *It's nicer.*

And I say, *Right.* And for a moment I've
gained an aura of one who's been.

Loose Threads

They seem connected,
if by nothing else than the space between.

She's stopped, on the verge
of giving up following, and in the middle
of the crosswalk

making her way behind him, shouts,
Carl, gimme back my clothes,

like no one else is in the crosswalk
or in the world, and I'm not
passing her going the other direction.

Her voice loud, cracking,
almost funny—the raspiness—but not,

more a tug at a loose thread.

It's cold. October. Gray.

So I'm not sure what she's doing in bare feet,
white, heavy set, wearing ratty jeans

and a T-shirt. I passed who I think is Carl
half a block ago, his rigid walk,
putting face and shoulder muscles, his mustache,

into shutting out everything around,
hands in jacket pockets.

I've never had to ask for my things back in a fight,
but that feeling

of getting left behind, like waiting
in an echoey hall.

I think about my friend,
his rough first year of marriage.

This neighborhood's changing.

The small wooden houses
and student apartments with flaking paint

replaced by luxury apartments
done in earth tones
and with porches that don't droop,

cinderblock bars
by brew pubs with restaurants, patios.

I prefer the newer places,

party to the loss
of what I thought I liked about this neighborhood,

about myself.
I'm letting the birds distract me.
Chimney swifts, surprised they haven't

migrated yet. Feeding on insects,
but their darting like darning a hole in the sky,

their chatter
hard to be around without harboring
a grain of hope.

I need to call my friend (it's been a while),
see if he's up for a beer.

With Time

I'm the one to hollow the pumpkin and carve a face.
The doorbell rings again. You adore the children
tonight in their costumes. A warm night.
We have no costumes, just the two of us
and the space between forming a shape we keep repeating.
My turn to go and hand out candy. We finally threw away
the photo from the booth that merged our faces,
a composite to show what a daughter of ours
might look like. She looked freaky not being real.
This isn't yours alone to carry, isn't your failure.
We won't let us drift apart, but there's nothing
to work on or figure out. With time you'll say
your body doesn't crave being a mother anymore.
You can't say it now, your silence
a place into which I don't know how to follow you.

Boys' Life

Myths and cautionary tales from parents,
children's retelling of them, their morphing,

don't eat the apple's core, the seeds poisonous,
will grow into a tree inside you, inside your eye,

the two boys old enough that what they want
to know is how to swear, to order from the back

of Boys' Life Magazine, X-ray glasses,
already curious about bodies, their smoothness,

smells, crevices, ways they're entered,
games of pretend to skirt around the edges,

or seeing, for real, what they can do
to their skins colliding with concrete,

falling from skateboards and bikes in alleys,
testing what they can throw and how far,

a letdown compared to the distance in their minds.
One has a new BB gun, a lemon on the neighbor's tree

within range, when hit giving up a tear.
And the dove on a low-hanging wire,

its abrupt fall to earth. This time
they've gone too far; but why?

Nobody saw them. The stupid thing just sat there
waiting to be shot. Already they're wishing

they could piece together what's been broken
and put it back the way it was.

Voices

Odd that since I was a boy, I've never felt the presence
of the dark until now, its sheer,
massive walls towering above me as though I've fallen

into a crevasse. What time is it?
From the hall, through a closed door, voices of nurses grow

louder then fade, becoming a murmur

like the murmur one hears in a breeze stirring sycamores
and roughening the surface
of a lake, in a stream of freeway traffic,

in waves breaking, the tide going out. Will it leave me?
It's quiet here. I dreamt

you were on a screened-in porch of a cabin talking
with your sister,
laughing sometimes, fireflies outside. I listened. Listening

was enough. In this dark, this quiet, I drift

from myself as though I'm
in the back row of an empty lecture hall, my body
on a table down in front—the subject

of a talk I slept through. What was said?
Weren't you there? I dangle my hand alongside the bed

as if dangling it in surf
washing up the beach. Will the water reach me,
the voices return?

From Within

Lake Monona, Madison, Wisconsin

Acolytes of the sluggish, muggy dark,
their dozen or so rods—the tip of one dipping
into the still water—crowded around a spot

where street runoff empties into the lake, Black
and Hmong anglers casting from shore, some sitting
on large plastic buckets, and white anglers from aluminum boats

they've brought in close, a ball game on a radio, bobbers
with lights like fireflies above the surface
though fireflies don't hover above surfaces

or bob but trace part of an arc like a match
as it's tossed away. Otis Redding's plane
went down here on the way to his next show.

I doubt he knew the name of the lake, his thoughts
other places when he traveled. If you walk
this path certain times of day, you'll notice

a loon close enough to see the red in its eye,
strange in the reflection of a power plant,
of four tall smoke stacks and a city skyline.

Have you caught a fish of any kind? From within
that stillness you feel a tug. At first you're not sure
what it is, your heart thumping in your chest.

Vista

Heat is heat, even if the air is less humid.
A ridge-line and hazy mountains in the distance
like offspring, children something to point to
as one's future, children out of the picture for us.
I don't feel inconsolable.
We can be ourselves to each other, which you'd think
would be enough but at times feels like nothing
when I say it, just the dry heat of the day,
grass, dirt, and needles on the ground, a hint
of sweetness in the air from the Jeffrey pine. We've hiked
around Mt. Wilson with views over the San Gabriels.
You're spreading out your arms the way I love it
when you do to say, *All this.* The vista
opening through you, you the frame.

On the Edge of Sleep

Small bells tied with ribbon
to black, leafless branches call out a swelling
and easing of a breeze. The wolf I was terrified of
sniffs me and wants to play, but what started
as a gentle drizzle gets heavier.
I don't want to get soaked and don't
know my way in the woods—the wolf
no help on that account. I'm without
whatever I usually carry
to and from places, whatever tasks
I typically have at hand. I've lost
my shoes again (where do they disappear to?),
have nothing to cover my head. And the taxi
that was meant to wait for me left.

Out of Nowhere

I can't tell if it's scared, the bat flying toward me
along the baking-goods aisle

level with my face, flapping like a wind-up toy

and effortless, not like a startled
mourning dove, no weight, no whistling of wings.

Then it's passed me, a blond
grocery clerk, a high school boy with acne
and an apron chasing it,

holding, with both hands, a box of Cheerios
above his head. Maybe you're smiling

at the image the way I'm smiling now, though

I'd have thought I'd feel
a little sadness too knowing what will probably

happen to the bat. It's here
and gone, something of its presence remaining another
moment after like an echo of a shout

that seems to come out of nowhere and goes unanswered
in a neighborhood at dusk.

Corner Store

Inglewood, California

If there'd been an Asian-American Norman Rockwell,
he might have painted a scene
like this. The Vietnamese shopkeeper with gray,

slicked-back hair and bony hands,
a baseball game on his small black-and-white TV.

And I, the white, dark-haired
nine-year-old in cut-offs sliding a coin across
the counter toward him.

The title of the painting might read *Debt Repaid*.
The shopkeeper's moved

that I've come back with the one cent I was short of

half an hour earlier
for whatever it is he let me buy. *You're a very
honest boy*, he says.

When I walk in twenty years later a Black college student,
earring in his left ear, sits behind

the counter doing school work, behind what looks
like bullet-proof glass.
So the store survived the riots. But the freezers

seem quieter, not that sound
of slow, steady rain. Or maybe it's just that I've grown.

And where did they put those bright
packages of Jaw Breakers,
lemon drops, Hot Tamales, and Bottle Caps I'd stand

in front of, touching each
before selecting one? Now I think of it,

I'm not even sure I know he was Vietnamese. And do I

really remember an urgency
in his voice, a sense something he's held on to

won't last, take root?
Very honest boy, he tells me with a weight, an adult
seriousness, the passion

embarrassing me so that I want to step outside
into the light, surround myself

with the ongoing diatribe of traffic noise, a jet coming in low,
and stuff my mouth
with a piece of colored wax in the shape

of lips, an oversized wad of gum, or those crystals, Pop Rocks,

that dissolve by producing
an odd, beautiful effervescence on the tongue.

Intimate Venue

Dakota Jazz Club, Minneapolis, Minnesota

Shades of hurt, reverberations of ice cracking,
how her voice still rings true
after all this time. Even the cutesiness in it

and a bowler hat she uses for a prop,
if pressed, we might admit they speak to us,
her stage presence

a real presence despite wrinkles around
her mouth and eyes, that tone
taking us back with her 30 years.

I'd play one of her tunes obsessively,
its hint of more around the corner
even if just absence, echo.

Then at some point I moved on
to other things. Tonight her best causes
an audible stir among us like we're a stream

spilling over a bed of rocks. I don't mean
her recent songs but her hits, those
marked by the glow of our phones

set to camera mode. We'll get it digitally,
that shot, the essence, each rip our personal chunk
from the loaf of bread that's this, here,

now, her, though by fidgeting we're missing
the urgent coursing through of it
like water toward the sea.

Cottonwood at Dusk

An onset of shadows, branches
and leaves going black, becoming their own absences

still rippling and swaying against
a fading gray-blue sky. Then the blackness spreading,
merging into clumps,

a young boy's shout caught up in shadow,

a few last leaves lifting
and falling before giving up their shapes entirely.

II. Doors Open and Closed

Sparrow

If this were a pond and she stood still in it
she'd be an egret. But she's
all small calculated moves,

her green cashmere sweater,
twenty-something youth,
shoulder-length blond hair

headed for the free sample of blue-corn
tortilla chips and guacamole, then clutching
a fistful of red, unwashed grapes, one bulging

in her cheek. At the self-serve island
of the deli section, black plastic tongs in hand,
she drops into the hollow

of her palm three wedges of potato
sautéed in rosemary,
barely stopping while she flits,

without basket or cart, among shoppers,
practiced in this space, hunting up what's to be found
along peripheries of vision

as if it were fallen seed in the shadows
of a tree-lined drive leading
to a great estate. Then she's gone,

having managed a small meal of it
without purchase or commotion, a glass door
shutting behind her like a sleepy eye.

Farther Than I Thought

Dusk, bare oaks across the street looking
less like trees, more like cathedrals
with their columns and vaulted ceilings,
echoes and saints, we changing too among

the day's last shadows, you at our living-room window,
lights off, chin resting on your knee,

like a passenger on a train, and I,
hunched over a book in the near dark,
either a fist opening or closing. I've read

people are meant for certain moments
they come into their own, stand out, like falling snow
when lit up by the headlight of a locomotive,
like anything all of a sudden there in the branches,

owl-eyed, or reflected in a river. Though
the afternoon you and I found ourselves
stuck in traffic between protesters
and police with their shields, helmets,
M16s, I just wanted to go unnoticed, slip
through the cordon to the other side. And once,

after a storm, not sure where the others
I'd come with had wandered, up to my knees

in a snow drift next to a stream, surprised
by a ram's horn I held, how it simply
broke off in my grip, the ram I was
trying to free still stuck, blood on its head
at the stump, night coming on, trees

in their moment of transformation, I suddenly
felt far away, a lot farther than I thought
I'd gone. I like the movie about a journey,
a tin man, wicked witch, something

the wanderers search for far from home, a wizard
who shows them what they've already become.

Rain

I've managed to keep up the newness
of arrival for so long, that habit of picking up
and moving a kind of forgetting and yet
when I step into the next thing
I find myself all the way back again, a cold
drizzly day in Minneapolis, the softening
and rot of fallen maple leaves taking me back
almost anywhere else I've been, D.C.,
Madison, Marburg, Oxford, even a wintery L.A.
My mother wonders if we'd stayed in Portland,
bought a house, settled instead of traveling
when my sister and I were growing up,
following the map of my father's
falling down and getting up,
his unfinished dreaming, preaching,
teaching, arriving and vanishing toward God,
what it would have been like. Rainy I imagine.

Altadena

Some streets curve. Not all the streets go through.
From a nearby stadium sounds
of a cheering crowd. You were going to teach;

I was going to be a house husband
and write. The man living with his mother
half a block away drank during

the day in a pickup he'd park by our house
while we were at work. He'd throw empties
underneath our oleander hedge. Everything

seems present and past at the same time.
Past tense like, *Remember how nights the city lights
glowed like embers*? Present like, *I wonder*

*if water still drips into the fireplace
when it rains.* Summers neighbors we never saw
drained their swimming pool into the street.

Parrots made a racket in the palms.
Exotic trees stained the asphalt
jacaranda purple, olive black.

After wind storms the litter of seeds, seedpods,
fronds. Jehovah's Witnesses, briefcases in hand,
at the front door. A family

of raccoons knocking over trash cans,
a clatter like they were playing.
A Ford Mustang waiting to be restored.

Coyotes trotting down the middle
of the road, dazed, as if they'd expected
to find themselves somewhere else.

Stairs that once lead to a hotel entrance
leading nowhere, just foundations remaining.
Low-hanging phone lines, insulation drooping,

blue sky tangled in wires.
Roosters, peacocks in people's yards.
Police helicopters. Once or twice gunfire

that seemed a safe distance away.
On clear days the ocean
a distant glint of sunlight through the trees.

High School Dance

N.E. Minneapolis, 1983

This yearbook photo's not as sharp, a hallmark
of the photographer. I was unsure
with camera lenses and adjusting
in a new setting, new school,

remembering other friends, another place.
If we're talking landscapes we return to
when distracted, mine's a path
through an empty field to the river's edge,

a place for trying cigarettes,
nothing you'd take a picture of.
In the photo no absent landscapes,
only Hmong teenagers wearing

fake-leather jackets, the nearest of the three boys
even shorter than his friends,
with a hunched, disfigured back,
and in mid-conversation, animated,

though I hadn't thought of him that way,
rather as quiet along with other refugees
from Laos who'd crowd a far corner
of the lunchroom, separate from the rest.

One can feel so seen or unseen and continents
away from what one knows, whether Hmong,
or Black—bused in from the other side of town,
whether one has lost or gained by the distance crossed,

and these three off to the side in a high school gym
hoping to meet someone, talk, maybe
even dance, saying by their presence,
postures, *Ready or not, we're here.*

Current

It runs through sleep, through deserts, through cellars.
The river bears me on and I am the river.
      —from "Heraclitus" by Jorge Luis Borges, translated by
      Norman Thomas di Giovanni

In sex ed, video of childbirth, or in drivers' ed
of car crashes, bloodied windshields,
not just images, but silences and sounds

making everything more real. Sometimes,
out of class, it's simply my thumb sliced open
after falling on a stair, an appalling quiet,

feeling myself pulled deeper into the wound.
The first trick—remembering to breathe. The second,
not letting the current catch me,

the tug always stronger than I think
(annoyed how easily I forget),
grabbing hold by focusing on anything else

before the dizziness sets in and sweeps me out,
my nose and cheekbone hit the floor,
the sting of the impact

lingering when I wake. Eventually
I'll build on a skill I already have, useful
not just for this but other situations,

putting distance between myself
and what I see, instead of feeling
a scalpel I'm watching on the big screen

like it's my chest under the knife,
cut lengthwise, the inner cavity exposed,
turning away, keeping myself whole.

Dana Point

People watched us from the breakwater
as if we were on display. The washed-up kelp stank,
flies covering it.

I picked up a stone, put it in my pocket, some
sudden need to possess or connect.

A father skipped
the ones he found, showing off I thought
though I don't know why.

The mother looked on from a blanket,
their toddler busy

picking up stones as well.
You were envious of the woman, I know,
but I said nothing,

nothing left for us to say. We got on the boat

we'd come down for,
saw a pair of whales, glimpses

of their barnacle-covered backs,
then a pelican almost skimming the ocean.
And started to enjoy ourselves.

The dolphins, melancholy
or sedate, didn't ride the bow waves

the way they often do
but ignored us instead, arching
their dorsal fins out of, into the water

like sprockets turning
on a gradually forward-moving wheel.

One would cross over
behind the rest as though weaving together threads
left in their wakes. The boat,

in keeping pace with them, barely moved.
We could hear their breathing.

People came to the rail with cameras.

Then, as if on cue,
the dolphins disappeared.

By the Tracks

They don't know, beyond a certain point
in either direction, where the tracks lead,
the railroad bed an open, empty swath
through their neighborhood
past the brick, whitewashed warehouse,

community gardens, a few sycamores,
a rusted Studebaker in the grass waiting
to be restored, a camper top on cinderblocks.
Their neighbor who wears plaid wool shirts
once threw a brick at the locomotive.

If the train's too much to take
they wonder why the neighbor moved there,
the crossing and bridge at either end
bordered by buckthorn where the tracks
disappear like a question, every few hours

an answer, even occasionally during the day
the wave of an engineer, and again quiet.
They've not only gotten used to it
but have come to need the hugeness of its passing
to sleep through the night, the newlyweds

snug spooning between comforter and futon,
windows shuddering, a deep throb entering
and leaving their dreams, a beast through a forest,
the sound, as if from the back of a throat,
hollow and full, calm on the verge of fury.

Called

Then who's that wandering by the porch
again and calling us by name?
    —from "March Elegy" by Anna Akhmatova, translated by
    Stanley Kunitz and Max Hayward

There's the way friends find him despite himself,
show up unannounced at his place, others

than the ones he thought would end up
as his friends, asking him to look

at a used car with them or come to Target because
they're going. And his reflection in storefronts,

echoes of his steps in hallways
of malls, conversation about him he overhears

at a party, all not what he expected,
versions of himself but not quite him

or more so, snippets taken, altered, remixed
as if by a DJ and thrust out. Like hearing

himself in songs, but the moments of recognition
more sudden, raw, the blood welling from a cut thumb,

a rancid smell from fish slime smeared on his jeans,
the call of a couple of geese foraging in the mud

of a half-flooded field, piercing, going through him
like he's air. And the refinery on the river, its empty catwalks,

ladders, smell of sulfur, of burning and decay,
the continuous open flames prayers

for the future, though the choices have already been made,
whatever was to be done is done.

Search

Altadena, California

I don't hear the helicopter until it's overhead,
the whole house shuddering around me.
As quickly as it's come it's flown on

toward the hills, a heavy wop wop
of turning blades still echoing. If even
small events have meaning then the message

of this is simple—*Be quiet and listen.*
Not everything's about you—the way
a stray dog wandering down

the wet streets of our neighborhood
isn't about me, rain running off of papery leaves
of a eucalyptus, rain leaking

into our fireplace, rust-colored drops.
The TV news covers a father and son
lost in a canyon,

the temperature dropping, their absence,
the helicopter sent to find them,
like a pause in conversation, anticipation

of an answer, like an empty room
in which I notice my footsteps, glad
it isn't me gone missing.

Contingencies

If we ever need a roof to get up on,
say during a flood, we've got one, though
I'm not sure what we'd do after that.

If we need firewood,
say it's below zero, the heat goes out
and there's nothing else,

at least we've got the furniture
and a fireplace to burn it.
Grab the photo album and flash drive

if the house goes up in flames.
That face of yours, the one you make
when giving me a fake scowl.

I'll capture it with my phone's camera
to cheer me when I'm overcome
by boredom, defeat.

If nothing else, we have
our memories of good times
to keep our heads above water,

family, friends, trips, what we picked up
along the way (acorns, feathers, rocks),
conversations, maybe not so much

the words anymore but how
people we remember might have said them.
A tone. What they'd say now

were they here to say it.

Spoken Word

You, the one in front of the audience
and with a voice for it, clearly pronouncing, no hesitation or hurry,
into a microphone—sound converted to electricity,

language of the universe, and back
to sound, amplified—speak to us, offer
fragments of your life as testimony, prayer.

Tell how a cloud had a silver lining, and it'll resonate,
calling up for me a time my wife and I stood on the deck
of a whale-watching boat while it headed

past the breakwater, light around dark edges of sky
though a cold wind kept up; gray, swelling waves;
on-again-off-again drizzle. Through your visions

speak for us. Say in your own words
how I'd lose myself in books about mythologies
I don't believe. She'd get lost looking at historical photos,

always wanted to know the context, what's beyond
the frame. Say I left yesterday without my wallet.
Say we had the right intentions, weren't

that far off searching for a remnant
of prairie, bison in the distance, something
timeless to connect with, weren't close either,

the bison scattered on the hills like spilled raisins,
not many of them, not really timeless at all.
Mention the train conductor looking up

right when we looked down at him, then the freight train,
its weight, its thunder passing under us
and the bridge we stood on like we were the eye

of a needle being threaded. Record each testimonial
so we can play it again—words converted
to stored memory, memory back to words.

Finding Each Other

the fact of your body
stretched out on the top sheet
as present as a city block
on a cool
cloudy morning

your short gray-and-brown hair

freckles along your sides
star clusters on your midriff
celestial maps

valleys running along the ridges
of your hip bones
crooked toes
remnants of nail polish

everything a given
shadow and light
doors open and closed
dead ends
and alleys you can't see the end of

that after all these years
you're still shy about it

that when we find each other
it's as if by accident

try not to move for a moment
so i can look at you

The Way Things Come Together

I wonder who the limousine is for, the one
below with headlights on

in the middle of an empty parking lot. Why

the bar with stools in this otherwise
ordinary hotel room? With someone else, a friend,

I could joke about it,
make it a topic of conversation, how it gives
the place a '50s feel. My copy

of Whitman beside the bed seems lost,
not just the worn

paperback on a spotless glass table,

but the poems inside, the sweep of them, what's
brought together there.
I could joke about the salesmen

at the meeting I flew here for,
their polo shirts, cologne, after-dinner drinks, cigars,

but that would be smug.
They seemed alright, seemed to know themselves,
their place. I've always

told myself I'll live in the present, watch,

listen for patterns, the way
things come together, though often
nothing happens.

III. Water's Edge

Joe

I came for the quiet, the conversation.

All evening you've returned to the story of a man you loved
who didn't love you, or who loved you
but couldn't stop loving others. This archeology,

sorting of shards, searching for a whole.
It seems late in the year for crickets. There's an ongoing

murmur from the freeway, cars on I-90 headed for Beloit,
Rockford, Chicago,
you after work counting cards out loud, fifteen two,

fifteen four, a pair for six,
moving a peg around a cribbage board, me with my cards,

fifteen two, fifteen four, the kitchen door

open a crack to let out the cigarette smoke, the air cold,
the moon just above the horizon, huge,

weighed down like a loaded barge, night with its chaos
of barking dogs, your voice
a thread holding things together, a virus in your blood

trying to undo you
like fingers working away at a knot. Joe,

don't judge yourself. This afternoon
I walked down State Street with shoppers and students,
their shadows touching, a man

with an overcoat, gray beard, and earrings playing harmonica
on a park bench, singing the blues, teenagers

on corners in baggy jeans, cigarettes between thumb
and forefinger, giving each other
bored, knowing looks, a preacher, bible in one hand,

pointing with his other, store windows

with their oversized photos of fashion models, images
of happiness like bright, fluttering kites.

Nicaragua

I don't remember when the indignation started to seem stale,
self-righteous. And the rhetoric.

What I do remember of those times is a protest sign with the word

tomorrow misspelled—two Ms
and only one R. It made me feel silly being

part of the crowd. So I went home.
But years later that I'd have this sense of loss
like an empty banquet hall, a curtain

billowing in the breeze of an open window. What of the people
brought together? Of knowing

something for certain? And you, Pippa. You hoped to go down,

help out. There were things to do,
literacy campaigns, public health drives, schools
that needed building. You

wanted to use your hands for more. And have a child. Did you make it
to Nicaragua?

Starting Again

The moon grows fuller from right to left
and its spreading darkness too

later in the month from right to left—
things I'm discovering.
The sun came up this morning

in the glass of downtown and for a moment

I thought of all of us
as windows of flame before the sky dulled again.
You're quieter, having a harder time

just being though there's nothing out of the ordinary to point to,
maybe because,

and I'm not helping much.
A transplant from L.A., enamored of the Midwest,
you always find ways to celebrate

the seasons, picking up a red leaf from the sidewalk,

placing it as a centerpiece
on the dining-room table. I give you a kiss on the mouth

as a way of avoiding answering
your question. You asked what I was doing
when I got out of bed last night

to jot down a note in pencil. I was starting again,

seeing what I can
piece together by naming one thing I know
so later I can add to it another.

Happy Hour

I want to sleep with her.

An algorithm her doctor's run says she has an increased
chance of cancer; no real reason

to think she's got that now,
but the thought quiets me like I'm set back
from the scene.

We're having drinks with two of my coworkers.

I've ordered buffalo chicken wings
so she'll eat something

but end up eating most of them myself.
She's unassuming.
They've looked forward to talking with her.

I let them, only throw in
a few words of my own, get into my second glass.

We don't have kids. They're mothers;

one scheduled a babysitter.
They're talking about books they're reading.

Sometimes she'll ask me
to read her a poem at night, not one of mine
though she likes what I write,

but by anyone else to calm her mind
so she can sleep.

Between Shifts

His upcoming day of wooden and plastic pallets,
machine operators, loading docks, safety first,
16 dollars an hour, predictable conversation
likely starting with *Whatchya doin' this weekend?*
Leading to gun calibers, sex,
to, *Just married are ya?—still gettin' some then.*
Mall-photo-booth pictures in wallets,
families—new, broken up, adopted.
The idea of writing about it to him
a kind of boasting or blunt instrument,
doesn't pull one deeper into anything.
But he knows how, if he painted or really
knew how to use a camera he'd bring it
all together in the scene in front of him
this morning as he gets off the bus,
the leafless ginkgo a blackened outline
on an indigo, pre-dawn sky, a couple
of semi trailers unattached, the factory building
square as if no one had used any
imagination in designing it, just built
a monument to surrender, pairs of weak,
yellowish headlights in the parking lot,
steam from tailpipes, that moment
one shift's pulling out, the stragglers
of the next still pulling in.

Mrs. Engebretsen's Banquet, Glendorado, Minnesota, Eighteen Seventy-Something

I want to know what the Sioux thought of lutefisk.
I'm confused because her act

was one of kindness but unsettles me. Mrs. Engebretsen,

with her fjords, aquavit,
flat bread, Norwegian Bible, her New World,
setting a table with white linen

and silverware
for the half-starved Indians. I think of this

because it's what I'd do, or would want to, the ugliness
of need requiring some gesture.
There's the story of the Pentecost, people gathered to share

a meal, brought together by the act of remembering,
then the tongues of flame, everyone

speaking each other's language. I think of Mrs. Engebretsen

looking at her guests—strangers
living on the same land
but in their own lost landscapes—and not knowing

what to say to them, keeping
the conversation going with small talk.

Motionless

but as if ready for flight, next to the elevators
in an art deco office building, a bronze statue of a nude man
wearing a skullcap and with what could be propeller blades

or wings for arms, one pointing up, one down, gives the sense
of direction, purpose, if not grace, if a little strange,
a stern-faced hall monitor. Maybe because

we think ourselves haphazard but guided by fate,
foolish but right, we can, along with our opinions,
best intentions, friends, get on without much trouble

with the business of living, walk into a restaurant,
take our places, have lunch out. Outside the cold,
the ordinary noise of a city, and an empty, fenced-off lot

under a shroud of snow as if holy places reside
among the mundane, places not meant for us. The quote
about being doomed to repeat history comes up at our table,

each of us a Cassandra or voice in the wilderness, each of us
speaking of different parts of the past. In the background
a city clock striking the hour. A character in an unfinished

Kafka novel says we try too hard like a child tugging
at a tablecloth, bring the things we wish for crashing to the floor.
I've seen a character with long hair and a wool cap

step into traffic, bring it to a halt, a Moses dividing the Red Sea,
as if making a point in front of a stopped fire engine,
its lights and siren going, as if he was the point,

had nothing else, no other card to play. You too
have inner ruins, dark places you step out of. At least that's what
came to mind when, all of us gossiping about someone

who often broods and once, by accident, lit himself on fire, you,
unlike the rest of us, spoke of him without judging and so left
an impression on me like a bronze statue in an office building,

odd, intent, verging on elegance, or the tattoo of a jay in flight
on a waitress's forearm, or the imprint of a small bird's wing-beat,
wing and tail feathers fanned in the snow of a fenced, empty lot.

Graffiti

Minneapolis, Minnesota

Words and initials on bridge girders like leaves
blown together along a fence. *Bebop,*
BKP, Blink, Boozer, Maven, Lone,

Enter, STS. Noise of freeway traffic
crossing the river. Song of sparrows.
We walk down to the water. You once found

a gnawed-off claw and wing of a young hawk
along the fence of our yard. When you told me
and I went to look, the wing had disappeared

without any sign of the culprit, the claw
in snow by itself like a slash in a bus seat
or a scarf on an empty stage after a play,

the story over, actors and audience gone.
When my time comes I'd like to think I won't
be scared, could let go of the urgency

to be someone, of trying to find the right words,
though I remember feeling panic once,
calling out in the dark from my bed, no one

hearing me, no one answering. People scrawl anything
on anything, on these limestone cliffs, on trees
and buildings to claim turf, claim they were here,

belong, would scrawl on the sky if they could, the daylight
seeping through cloud cover distilled, distant, a word
like a wing. What should we belong to,

call ourselves, the gray sky losing light now,
tracks of geese leading across a patch of snow
and the sand of the riverbank to the water's edge?

Going Back

Inglewood, California

There's always one
who's rumored not to bathe or wear clean underwear,
sacrificial, defining others

by being what they're not. I forget her name, but she
took it on, her role, made a game of it

by touching us, *giving us her germs,*
about the only way she could belong, one of just four
or five whites in the school, like me,

the rest Black, though that alone didn't seem to be
an issue. At least I didn't notice

being treated differently. I and maybe ten boys had a game

of racing up and down the playground
like a motorcycle gang, our hands held out and gripped

around imaginary handle bars,
voices making engine sounds, growling, revving, forged together,
childlike I'm sure

but coming back to me as a roar.
The playground and school look just the same now,

though more run down
than I remembered them. And in the neighborhood,
again occasional clusters of people

sitting, talking on front steps, but more of them Hispanic,

even fewer white. And there,
the house I lived in. It used to have a fennel plant
out front we'd pull

branches from and chew, its licorice taste still lingering.
Hidden, what I'd like to see most,

half a mind to go up to the house and knock,
is, or used to be,
a garden, the kind that stays

with one, honeysuckle,
ivy, a sprawling century plant, foxtails

that'd get caught in the ankles of one's socks,
a swing set and a shelter
with a picnic table, a place for birthday parties, friends,

and usually above it all a Jumbo Jet, low,

hanging almost motionless, its shadow
passing over us.

Stopping the car across the street I watch a teenager,
afro, jeans and a plain T-shirt,
come toward me down the drive, looking at me

like, *Who are you? You don't belong.*

Before Rising

And the spirit found outside its housing? It breaks.
...not fated to have at hand a way back.
—from "The Surviving" by Christopher Gilbert

I was sick enough they knocked me out
with drugs for a week, cut me open. In my dream
nothing needed to be done or explained,
everything I was seeing seen from the sky
looking down through beating crows' wings.
I woke, wanted to call you, then wasn't sure
what I'd say. Did Lazarus,
when drawn into consciousness again
like a drop of water into cloth, feel
gravity's weight, hesitate before rising?
If I were to stand outside a room now,
hear talking, I might pause, listen before entering,
joining in. If I recognized you
in the crowd of shoppers and students on State Street
I'd probably hold back before waving or let you
pass by altogether without catching
your attention. Don't take it the wrong way
when I tell you this. I've been in a room
with voices, with your voice, after you've left
outside sounds filling it in your wake,
sparrow chatter, a locomotive's
low throb. This morning I could just as easily
spend my time on a park bench in shadows, listen
to the feet of walkers walking to work,
a breeze picking up, newspaper lifted into a spiral,
let go. I wouldn't need a voice.

Water's Edge

Mississippi River, Minneapolis, Minnesota

I wanted to see more than just the view
from above, from the bench,
part jogged, part slid, almost fell

coming down from the bluff into the gully,
dirt loosening under my feet.

Given the river seems still,

how quick the current
when I watch a branch swept along,

the flow not just the river moving
but a larger shearing in the landscape, an intention,
a kind of love or indictment.

You wouldn't have humored me

if you'd walked with me. And I'm not sure
what I was expecting anyway.
A crew team gets into its rhythm,

makes itself a loosed arrow on the water.
And the lapping wake of a motor boat

that's out of sight, the running of a motor
still within hearing.
Cigarette filters,

plastic bottles, and dirty froth
washed up on the sand.

Below street-level.
Entranced and on edge. A tug, not the breeze,
but as if I'm getting drawn

into an eddy and left behind.

And I've just spotted
a mattress in the brush with the remains of a campfire.
Thinking I should really be heading

back up, the shadow in this stand of trees
suddenly more present, lived in

or living among, pierced
by the call of birds and insects I can't name
and shafts of fading sun.

IV. A Sense of Space

'71 Monte Carlo

It's not her real car,
the brown Chevy pickup leaning to one side like one side of a face

gone slack, windshield cracked,
rust stains on lug nuts, along wheel-wells and doors.
The gear shift on the steering column sticks.

There's a trick to it—and opening the driver's door,
the idling engine loud,

sputtering, guttural, the woman I work with thirty,

plaid wool shirt over a T-shirt,
muddy boots, jeans, I with my own plans, a ponytail,

impatient to be somewhere,
listening in my empathetic, distracted way
without quite relating

to what she's saying, the car she'll get
when she has money, after the baby comes (though

the father's left), a '71 Monte Carlo,
candy-apple red with gold metal flake, black
crushed-velvet interior, Eagle GT tires,

Center Line Mag wheels, Munroe shocks, red lights
in the wheel-wells, a Muncie

four-speed transmission, and a 350 V8 engine (with a Holley

650 double-pumper carburetor,
Edelbrock manifold, Manley aluminum connecting rods,

high-compression aluminum pistons)
tuned so well you won't hear it when it idles, though you'll hear it
for sure when you hit the gas.

Crossing Nevada

The headlight of a train I'm watching
through open blinds never gets any closer.
The last light eases out of the day,

Ingrid Bergman and Humphrey Bogart on TV.
Next to our hotel, a Ferris wheel
spins an invisible thread. You love old movies,

the man with a white suit jacket and bow tie,
with a past like a trunk he can't put down,
the woman's beauty sharp as broken glass, the expanse

between them fraught with barroom tables,
conversations, half-finished drinks, how the two
find their way, planets falling into orbit.

You step out of the shower, your body
fresh as a manzanita after a good rain.
What am I worried about? Cars make their way

along the highway, eyes following eyes
into blackness. There's so much space, so much
numb distance, numbered doors lining

empty hallways, the ice machine's sharp thunder,
hours settling into their folds while in casinos
people drift like paper boats on separate ponds.

Moab

The others, some of them German and Japanese tourists,
drift up in small groups

toward the parking lot,
a few, college-aged, pushing each other around
for fun on the way.

I'm headed down the path toward the desert.

Shadow and orange rock.
The wind's died,

beauty this door to walk through.

I haven't given myself enough time though,
come at dusk, stopping
on the way somewhere else.

The farther I walk the fewer people I pass
until I'm the only one.

On my right, this expanse, maybe coyotes
and petroglyphs somewhere out there,
but all I see are darkening clumps of sage brush.

To my left these huge formations.

I walk up to one,
put my hand on it,

think of a few hundred million years,
feel and hear nothing
except the rock's coolness.

I should really go.

The orange has faded; sun's set.
If I don't turn around and get a move on now
I won't be able to find my way back.

Night Sky Without Meteor Shower

Years ago in Wisconsin I saw a whole field of fireflies,
this two-thousand miles away

and more ghostly, the yellow and white city lights below
seeming to dance
though they're not moving, but then that abrupt darkness

at the coastline. I'm in our backyard,

jeans pulled on over PJ bottoms,
bare feet, my neck tired from looking up, ordinary night sky

not what I expected
(Did I miss it? What time did the paper say the shower would start?)
though I wasn't sure what to expect

and, for that matter, I'm not what I expected,
how one thing leads to another,

an interconnectedness that feels it could easily

come undone, threads
like a grade-school project of loosely woven, hand-dyed wool

and a few stems of grass
added for effect, the melody of an ice cream truck in my head
since late this afternoon,

a deposit slip in my pocket, a recollection from earlier in the day
of a small omission,

a door not held open in haste or distraction,
also an old memory
of the dark as massive, like a crevasse

I'd fallen into; another time how it seemed a well

to draw from. And though still
no meteor shower, there's a quiet to the city I hadn't noticed before

like breathing, an on-again-off-again
rustle of eucalyptus leaves, some other background noise
like surf though not the surf,

then the whine of a small car with a loud muffler accelerating
as it fades into the night.

Undercurrents

The motives of crows on branches
when they silently bob their heads, or when they flock,

ash flecks on the wind.
Far away destruction that's still near enough
to want to distance myself from,

explain, be for or against, the country one

I hadn't thought about
until the war struck there like a single,
sharp clap of hands,

startling even if expected.
Today I've walked instead of driven, shadow

below a freeway overpass,
cooler air not warmed by morning sun,
the shudder above

of cars and trucks an uneven cadence

that makes me pause,
nothing else but sidewalk
and pigeon droppings,

not a place for gathering or conversation,
and no sign

of the man who circulates among traffic
stopped at the light, the one who sells gum, roses,
and bags of oranges.

Seizure

The edges giving way
not just spaces between things
anymore but space

my mother's voice not her at all
from deeper down or farther out
that thump of her when she's flung back

as if by high voltage from the dinner table
my eight-year-old self wanting
to catch her before she lands

the parakeet out of its cage
the cage knocked over
my sister and I without a clue

to let her sleep though it doesn't seem
like sleep more like she's been taken
and we're left behind

my father who's seen it all before
checking because she's stopped flailing
to make sure she's not biting

or swallowing her tongue
covering her with a wool blanket
leaving her on the floor for now

Gathering

Wobbly as if drunk but driven, following something,
whether freed or consumed by it,
small butterflies move through the city.

It's March. They're all around, flickers of orange

and black, part of a migration.
Men in straw hats or baseball caps wait for work

at street corners, some
sitting on the curb, some standing. They too seem
like they're hoping to arrive,

like cottonwood seeds
in air. Then evening, and it's the young in parking lots

of pizza places, fast-food restaurants,
teenage girls in twos or threes tentatively glancing
over their shoulders at boys,

the boys pretending not to notice, clustered

around souped-up Hondas,
leaning down to talk to friends inside.

Emerging

He couldn't read, hadn't for a year,
which in itself seemed a kind of death

given who he'd been,

Tillich, Bonhoeffer,
the Bible (in German and English), also
Louise Erdrich and Iris Murdoch the pages
my father used to get caught up in.

It bothered me he didn't miss the loss,
often forgot to eat real food as well,

Good-n-Plenties, saltwater taffy, Tic Tacs,
Werther's Candies, popcorn
(lightly buttered, salted),
also ice cream, almost any flavor,

what he'd hunch over
late, late at night.

I thought clarity,
perspective come with age.

The bathroom looked the way it does now,
large, clean,

but grown too large,
too clean given his new shape,
a pellet of bones
and yellowish flesh.

I'd help him off the toilet seat
or floor, expecting any moment
his curved spine to poke, white,
glistening, through his skin.

Once, for a few days and about a month

before he died, his mind
cleared and saw again

meanings in sentences

the way, through a short break in clouds,
before it pulls back, the sun
reaches down to touch the sea.

Third Street

Santa Monica, California

Musicians, sellers of cheap jewelry, of incense,
sketchers of pictures,

sleepers on benches, dancers and performers,

the one with a bowler hat,
his face painted silver, moving like a robot

to the beat of the music,
topiary shaped like dinosaurs, frat boys in dresses
for some kind of initiation

or a dare—all seem conspirators in an emptiness
you feel, things hoped for

that haven't work out. Even in this silence of yours

I'm taken by you, a little
afternoon light remaining, this place reminding me
of somewhere I can't quite recall,

only a few blocks' walk to see the ocean,
if you want to.

Viewing Reagan's Casket

Simi Valley, California, 2004

I want to believe in America. I've always
wanted to believe

completely, without doubt. But what I keep

returning to, what I've experienced,
thought, felt, ends up

sounding less like belief, more like loss,
desire. Even in your coffin
(strange, my disappointment

that it's closed) I'm sure you're looking at me

sternly, disapprovingly.
I don't know why I've come.

Sacred Heart

More curiosity in his face than anything else,
not what I'd expect

with a religious statue, fingers pointing
to the top of his tunic,
head bent down to look, an expression

that seems to say, *There's a hole in my chest.*

Interesting. Is the greater surprise
how his heart's magically appeared for anyone

to see or the meaning
of the crown of thorns around it as if love
is always bound by pain?

Objects

This jar of nails from my grandparents' basement becoming
just another jar of nails, maybe

that's what my father's afraid of, why he's kept it so long

after they died
though my mother's begged him to throw it out along

with the other things he's saved
and doesn't use. Maybe he knows how objects depend on us,
lose their meaning without us like a balloon

losing buoyancy, hovering closer to the ground in the corner
of a child's room.

Eight Floors Up

Only the tired end of a street, an empty schoolyard
like a shut eye, and apartments, windows
with squares of sky or the sky a mosaic of glass, something

to break with a well-thrown rock. You left an hour ago
and the room is still fresh with you, minutes
drifting downstream, sheets in their natural turmoil,

their landscape of gullies and rifts. We never
really have loved ones the way we have a stone
to hold in a moment of distraction, to know

the grain of. They slip through our fingers, beads of mercury
following gravity. In your wake the day washes back
into my life, transformed, hawthorn blossoms all over the street,

a nine-year-old in a neon jacket, hair in cornrows, threading herself
through a hole in the schoolyard fence, gulls
taking on a sudden whiteness against the coming storm.

Acknowledgments

Thanks to the editors and staff of the following publications in which the poems listed below first appeared, sometimes in different versions.

AGNI Online—"Mrs. Engebretsen's Banquet, Glendorado, Minnesota, Eighteen Seventy-Something"
Chelsea—"Voices"
Cider Press Review—"With Time"
Georgetown Review—"The Way Things Come Together"
Knockout—"Cottonwood at Dusk"
Lake Region Review—"Objects"
The Laurel Review—"Viewing Reagan's Casket"
MAYDAY Magazine—"Boys' Life" and "Called"
Pleiades—"Crossing Nevada"
Poetry Northwest—"Sparrow" and "Altadena"
Prairie Schooner—"Eight Floors Up"
Rattle—"Corner Store"
Southern Poetry Review—"Out of Nowhere" and "Dana Point"
TAB: The Journal of Poetry & Poetics—"From Within" and "Farther Than I Thought"
Tulane Review—"Joe" and "Nicaragua"

Special thanks to *Poetry Northwest* and Vandal Poem of the Day (VPOD) for featuring "Altadena" on the VPOD website. Also to TAB for nominating "From Within" for a Pushcart Prize.

I'm grateful to many friends who encouraged me when I needed it, in particular Catherine Baumgartner, Jil Evans, and Kris Woll. All three gave me valuable feedback on earlier manuscript versions. Thanks to David Bowen for his practical writing and publishing advice—and passion, which lifts up those around him, me included. Also thanks to Shuly Cawood and Robert McCready for being great literary citizens and sharing my work on their sites. Though I've been out of the classroom setting a long time, former teachers Jonis Agee, Phillis Levin, Michael Collier, Stanley Plumly, and Philip Pullman have remained inspirations. It still amazes me how their words and encouragement find their way back to me years later. I'm deeply grateful to all those at Finishing Line Press for whom getting so many voices out into the world is a labor of love. The love of my sister,

Ellen, mother, Arline, and memory of my father, Merlyn, sustained me in writing these poems. Finally I couldn't have finished this collection without Lian Partlow, not just center of my universe but repeat reader and honest, loving critic of all my work.

Brian Satrom grew up in Oregon, Germany, California, and England. His poems have appeared in a variety of journals including *Cider Press Review, The Laurel Review, Poetry Northwest, Rattle,* and *TAB,* which nominated his work for a Pushcart Prize. He has also published book reviews at *MAYDAY Magazine* and *Colorado Review.* He attended Macalester College in St. Paul and completed an M.F.A. at the University of Maryland, College Park. After living for extended periods in Madison, Wisconsin, and Los Angeles, he now makes his home in Minneapolis. His website is briansatrom.com.

www.ingramcontent.com/pod-product-compliance
Lightning Source LLC
Chambersburg PA
CBHW031044110426
42740CB00048B/1092